D1737118

About the Book

Summer had come to the Arctic tundra. A snowy owlet was hopping about in the grass, watching his father catch lemmings. All at once he saw a fox. It was hiding among the rocks and plants of the tundra, waiting to catch him. It was very close! The owlet saw the hungry mouth open, and he made a great effort. He raised his wings and jumped as high as he could. Then he ran shrieking toward the hill where his father sat. The big owl took off and swooped at the fox. The owlet had escaped!

In a few years, the young owl will have a mate and family of his own to protect. But before that time comes, he will have many more adventures on the tundra and in the deep forest where he migrates to spend the long, dark winters.

Alice L. Hopf's lively biography, which relates the life cycle of a snowy owl from birth to maturity, and Fran Stiles' beautiful, authentic line drawings perfectly capture the spirit of this magnificent white bird.

G. P. Putnam's Sons · New York

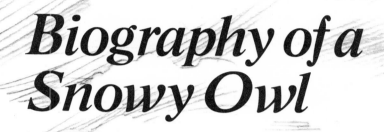

Biography of a
Snowy Owl

Alice L. Hopf

illustrated by Fran Stiles

Library of Congress Cataloging in Publication Data
Hopf, Alice Lightner.
Biography of a snowy owl.
"A Nature biography book."
Summary: Traces the life cycle of a snowy owl living
on the Arctic tundra.
1. Snowy owl—Juvenile literature. [1. Snowy owl.
2. Owls] I. Stiles, Fran. II. Title.
QL696.S83H66 1979   598.9'7   78-16533
ISBN 0-399-61130-4

for Penny and Pete and Andrew and Eric

Spring had come to the Arctic tundra. The snow was melting on the flat, treeless country that slopes down to the northern sea. Ice was breaking up. The streams were beginning to flow. Snow flurries still fell almost every day, but underneath the snow the grass was turning green. Early spring flowers poked up their heads. The days were growing longer.

The mother owl had made her nest on a low hummock, or rise in the earth. She had scooped out a shallow hole in the snow-covered grass and moss there. A thin lining of grass and feathers protected the eggs.

There were five of them in the nest, white and round with rough shells. The mother owl crouched down over them, spreading her feathers to keep them warm. Her body and wing feathers were mottled with dark streaks, but her face was pure white. The eyes in that white face were a bright golden yellow. When she settled herself on her nest and sank down into brooding position, two little tufts of feathers poked up above her eyes. But as soon as she sat up or left the nest, they disappeared, and her head was once more smooth and round.

As the mother owl sat on her nest, she was attacked by swarms of hungry mosquitoes. They gathered on her eyelids, the only spot where they could bite through her thick feathers. She shook her head to be rid of them, but they came right back. Sometimes she rubbed her eye against her shoulder, but still she stayed on her nest. The mosquitoes could not drive her from her eggs.

Now and then the female owl turned her head to watch the sky and tundra. She could turn her head almost all the way around and see in all directions. When she saw her mate coming, she began to grunt with excitement and bob her head up and down. The male arrived with a low, dipping flight. He landed beside the nest and held out a dead lemming— a small, mouselike animal—in his beak. He

was smaller than the female and almost pure white. His beak was black and his eyes glowed yellow.

The female took the lemming and began to eat, and the male flew off to hunt for more. She had been sitting on her nest for over a month and it was time for the first egg to hatch.

Owls begin to brood as soon as the first egg is laid. The eggs are laid several days apart, and the owlets hatch over a period of days. The babies are always different ages and sizes, and the oldest and biggest is likely to get more of the food.

The first egg hatched late in the day. The mother owl threw the pieces of eggshell out of the nest and soon was feeding bits of lemming to her new baby.

The young owlet was covered with white down. At first he was very weak and only poked his head out between his mother's feathers to get the food she offered. But in a few days he was able to stand. His eyes opened and he pushed out from under his mother and looked around. By this time another white, downy baby had hatched. When the owlet saw his father coming with food, he began to shriek. His mother stuffed food into his beak before she fed the younger baby.

As more eggs hatched, the female sometimes left the nest to help with the hunting.
The fluffy babies, lying on top of the un-
hatched eggs, kept them warm. But when the
mother was away, the nest was unguarded.

While she was robbing the nest of a smaller
bird, a hunting jaeger—a kind of gull—saw
the white down in the nest. It swooped down
for the prize. The baby owls were terrified.

The younger ones lay very still. But the first owlet hopped out of the nest and hid among some stones. His baby down had already changed from white to fluffy gray, and the jaeger did not see him. It grabbed one of the younger, white owlets and flew off.

The first owlet hid near the nest until his mother returned. Then he hurried to climb in and hide under her feathers. His mother was giving out food, and he opened his beak to get his share.

Perhaps the mother owl sensed that one of her babies had been stolen. She peered into the nest several times, but there was another egg hatching and the nest seemed full of downy chicks. She continued to brood and let her mate bring the food. Every four years the number of lemmings increases greatly, and in those years the owls find plenty of food for their nestlings. This was a good year for lemmings, and the mother owl did not have to leave her nest often to help her mate hunt.

The first owlet grew fast. He spent more and more time out of the nest. Now the snow was all gone, and the tundra was bursting with new life. The little owl hopped and ran about

in the grass. He watched his father, who often sat on a hummock observing the vast tundra around him. Only the head of the big owl moved, as he swiveled it slowly to keep everything in view. When a lemming or a ground squirrel came near enough to his hummock, the owl jumped down upon it. He hopped and jumped about in the grass, following every move of his prey till he could seize it in his

claws. Then he took the food to the nest where his mate was sitting. But often the first owlet ran after him, crying to be fed. Then the big owl would stop and give him some of the meat.

There were other enemies on the tundra besides the jaeger. The gull would never approach the nest if the female owl was sitting on it or if the male was on his hummock. But an Arctic fox was hunting nearby. She watched everything the big birds did. She had a den with babies in it over the next ridge, and she had to bring food to them. The fox had lost most of her white winter fur. Now she was gray streaked with black, and she blended in with the rocks and plants.

The first owlet had never seen a fox before. He was hopping about in the grass, watching to see if his father might catch another lemming. His young sister, the second owlet out of the nest, was following him. All at once the owlet saw the fox. She was very close! The owlet saw the hungry mouth open, and he

made a great effort. He raised his wings and
jumped as high as he could. Then he ran
shrieking toward his father's hummock.

The big owl took off and swooped at the
fox. But the fox had already pounced upon the
smaller owlet. She sat back and snarled at the
owl. The owl swooped down again. He hopped
angrily around the fox, spreading his wings
and clacking his beak. The fox grabbed the
owlet in her jaws and ran. She dodged among
the rocks and underbrush and escaped the an-
gry owl.

The first owlet ran and hopped back to the
safety of the nest. He climbed in and hid under
his mother's feathers. She was standing up,
grunting and hissing and clacking her beak.
But she stayed with her nest and let her mate
chase the enemy.

Summer was coming. Each day the sun stayed above the horizon longer, setting later and later in the day. Soon the sun would shine at midnight. Daylight would last for twenty-four hours.

Every day the first owlet grew bigger and stronger. More nestlings hopped out of the nest and joined him on the tundra. By the time the last nestling had found its way out, the first owlet had grown his flight feathers. He was learning to fly. He jumped up and down, opening his wings and waving them. Each time he flew a little farther.

Now the mother owl had left the nest. The
two big owls led their babies away across the
tundra, where the hunting might be better.
They kept on catching mice and squirrels and
lemmings to feed the owlets, but they also
taught them how to hunt for themselves.

The first owlet tried and tried to catch a lemming. He hopped and jumped after them in the grass. But the little animals were very quick. They scuttled into their burrows before he could catch them. At last the first owlet did what his father did. He climbed upon a hummock and sat perfectly still. He watched the ground carefully. He waited till a lemming was very close. Then he jumped. His claws closed on the furry body. He gave a quick squeeze to kill his prey, and he looked around to see if anyone challenged him. But the other owls were busy with their own hunting. He ate it all himself.

The first owlet now had all his flying feathers. He was not white like his father. He was not even as white as his darkly striped mother. His new feathers were all a mottled brown. Not until he molted—shed his outer feathers—the next summer would he be as white as his father. But he was learning to fly as well as the big birds.

Now there were more lemmings than before. The little animals seemed to be everywhere, and the owls all had plenty to eat. No longer did the owlet have to sit and wait for one to come close. The lemmings were running everywhere—a carpet of lemmings, going . . . going . . . going . . . they didn't know where.

Other predators came to hunt. Foxes followed the moving mass of lemmings, pounc-

ing here and there to catch a hasty meal. Jaegers and hawks came to the feast. Even wolves forgot about their larger prey and followed the swarm of little creatures.

The lemmings paid little attention to the predators. There were too many lemmings, and there was not enough food for all of them. They had to find a better place to live where there would be enough food. As they scampered on their way, they fed the many hungry creatures of the Arctic.

In two weeks the lemming migration had passed. Suddenly they were almost all gone. The owls followed the lemmings' old route, but it was hard to find a lemming to catch. And winter was approaching. The days were getting shorter. The sun no longer stayed above the horizon all the time. Twilight was growing longer and longer. Darkness and cold were coming again to the Arctic.

The parent owls began to move south, and their owlets followed them. Now food was harder to find and the owls spread out over a larger area. The first owlet lost touch with his parents, but he did not try to find them. Instinctively—without having been taught—he knew that each bird must have a larger hunting territory. He could find his own food now. He did not need his parents.

Instinct also told him to continue flying south. Other birds passed him in great flocks.

When he found no mice or squirrels on the
ground, the young owl swooped on a migrating songbird or duck. As he continued south-

ward he came to trees, and then more and more trees. Soon he was in a great forest. The trees made good lookouts, like the rocks and hummocks of his Arctic home. But the forest was so thick, it was hard to fly through it. It was harder to see the creatures he must catch for food. He had to learn to hunt in the dark.

Unlike most owls, the snowy owlet had lived his short life in almost constant daylight. He had learned to hunt under the midnight sun. But now he had to use his ears as well as his eyes for hunting. He learned to sit high on a tree branch and listen for the slight movement of a mouse in the leaves far below. Even on the darkest night, the young owl could locate the exact spot where his prey was by its sounds. He would swoop down on silent wings and strike with his great talons.

But the young owl was not used to the forest. He was used to wide-open country, and he searched for such a place. He passed villages and farmlands and cities in his southward travel. At last he stopped. He had found a wide, wide area with no trees. It was completely flat, like his homeland. All around the outside of the area was a fence that provided good roosting places. And inside was a vast expanse of snow-covered grass, full of the runways and nests of mice and other little creatures.

There were rabbits hopping about, and fat grouse and pheasants were busily eating the grass seeds. It was the best hunting ground the owlet had seen since he left the north. He settled down to make it his home.

There was only one thing wrong with the new territory. It had a number of long, narrow strips of grassless ground, and every now and then something huge, something bigger than anything the young owl had ever seen, would come roaring down and land on the grassless path. It made a terrible noise, and the first time he saw one the young owl was frightened and flew back to the trees a half mile away.

But the hunting ground was too good to be abandoned, and after a while he got used to the noise. The owl came back to sit on a fence post. Hunting was easy, and he had plenty to eat. He watched the airplanes come and go.

They even came and went at night. Soon he got so used to them that he ignored them. One evening he flew right in front of a plane that was taking off. He managed to dodge it just in time. The pilot also dodged and swore. It was a bumpy takeoff. He complained to the office.

"Get rid of that darned owl!"

The airport manager got out his gun, but his young assistant had a better idea.

"That's a young owl," he said, "and there's a law against shooting them now. I read about a man at the Toronto airport who traps them and then releases them far away where they can't get into trouble. Why don't we get him over here?"

The manager agreed. "But hurry up about it. We don't want to have an accident."

The man from the Toronto airport came with his traps. He set them out in the snow. The jaws of the traps were carefully padded with soft material so that the owl would not be hurt. The traps were baited with rabbits and birds. Then the man went away and waited.

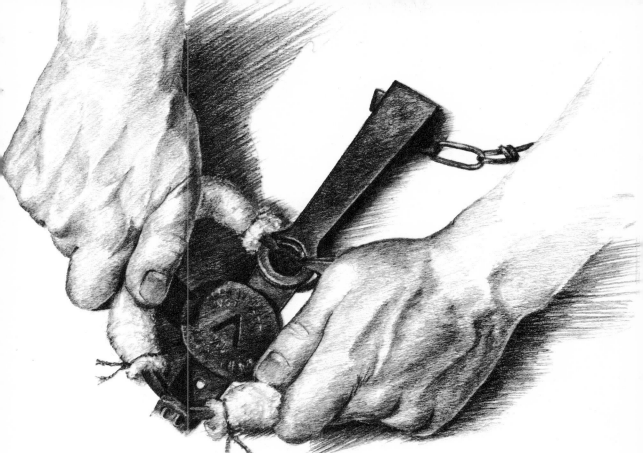

The young owl watched the man from his
perch on a fence post. He turned his head almost all the way around to keep him in view.
When the man had gone, the owl watched the
spot he had left. There was a rabbit there,
moving about on the snow. The owl took wing
and flew over the spot. It was a strange rabbit.
It did not run and hide as rabbits usually do.

But the owl was hungry. He swooped. His talons sank into the rabbit, and he started to fly away.

Just as he rose, his prey was snatched out of his claws. The owl was startled. He landed on the ground and hopped over to the rabbit. As he reached out with one leg to grab it, the other leg hit the trap. There was a loud click and the padded jaws closed on the owl's leg.

The man had kept watch from a distance, and when he saw the owl was caught, he came over to the trap with his assistant. The young owl lay on the ground and stared at the men, but he made no effort to fight or get away. He was terribly frightened. He let the man pull a sack over his head and tie his legs together.

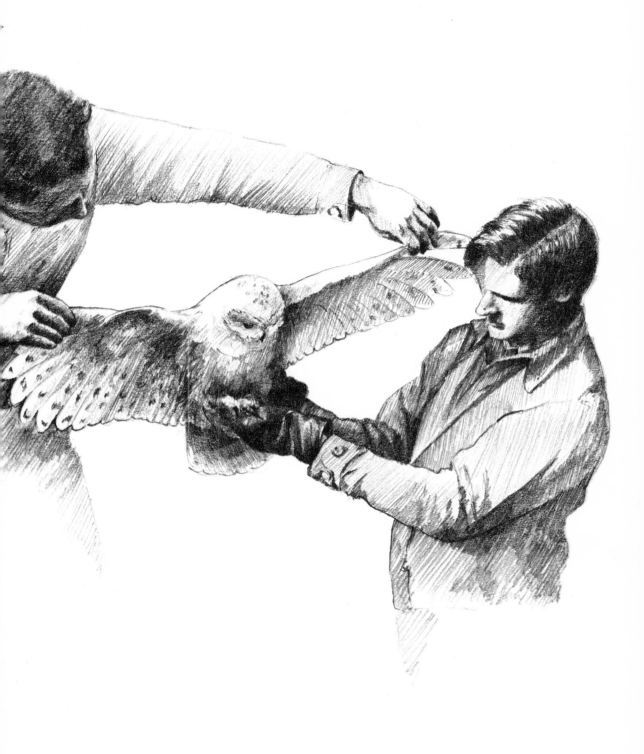

"A beautiful bird," said the man. "And his leg isn't even scratched. I'll just put a band on it so we'll know him if we find him again. And then he's going on a long ride, miles and miles away from any airplanes."

The man released the owl in a national park, where there were big lakes and deep forests.

At first the owl lay on the ground, not understanding that he was free. But when the man stepped back, the owl opened his great wings, and with scarcely an effort he was in the air and gone.

"Good hunting, owl!" called the man. "And a long life."

The owl stayed in the park forest until spring. The days were growing longer and he was restless. He watched other birds swinging north in long lines, and he drifted slowly after them. Now and then he caught one of the migrating birds for his dinner. He kept flying north.

At last the trees were far behind and he saw the flat tundra stretching before him. The owl knew instinctively that he was home. This was his country.

Now the sun was in the sky almost all the time. Other owls were sitting on hummocks everywhere. They were calling with a deep, booming sound that could be heard for miles. The young owl found a hummock and began to hoot, too.

Soon he grew hungry and went off to hunt. As the owl flew about, looking for food, he saw a female owl sitting on the ground. She had scooped out a shallow nest, but she was not working at lining it. She scratched a little and then she sat in the sun. The young owl came up to her and began to bob up and down. He lifted his wings and tail. He made little cooing sounds. He croaked and whistled. The female closed her eyes and seemed to sleep.

Instinct told the young owl that he should have brought a lemming. But this year lemmings were hard to find. He hadn't seen one for days. He came back with a piece of dead fish, but the female owl was not interested. This time she got up and left her nest. She flew away and hunted for herself. The young owl looked at the deserted nest that would never have eggs. He ate the fish himself. This year he would raise no young.

There were few snowy owl nests in the Arctic that summer. Very few owlets were raised, and the parent owls had trouble finding enough food for them. In time, the young owl molted. His new feathers were almost all white. He was a beautiful bird.

When the days grew shorter once more, he moved south. He had no family to travel with. He spent his second winter in the national park where he had learned to hunt in the bountiful forest. He was a solitary bird—he lived and hunted alone.

Once again spring came to the northern countries. Once again the owl made the long trip back to the tundra, drifting along with the great flights of migrating birds. But this year things were better for the snowy owls. There were more lemmings running about the tundra. The owl found a good hummock to sit on and began to make deep booming calls. From all around he was answered by other male owls, each trying to attract a female.

One day, as he flew about the still snow-covered tundra, the owl saw a female sitting on her nest. She was scratching out a hollow, every now and then pausing to turn around and make sure that it felt right. The owl dropped down in front of the nest. He lifted

his wings. He bobbed up and down. The female stared at him for a few minutes, but then she went back to pulling bits of grass and moss from under the snow and arranging them in the nest.

Instinctively the owl knew what he must do. He flew away, and in a short time he was back with a lemming in his beak. Now he danced up and down in front of the female. He swung the lemming back and forth invitingly. All the time, he was whistling and croaking to encourage her. The female stopped

fussing with her nest and leaned forward with interest. When he put the dead lemming down next to her, she picked it up. The male owl flew away to find another. This year the hunting was easy. When he had brought her several lemmings, the female accepted him, and the two mated.

Soon there was an egg in the nest, and a few days later there was another. The snowy owl watched as the clutch of white eggs grew. He guarded them carefully. He brought food to his mate, and when she left the nest he stayed nearby. He protected the nest against jaegers and foxes.

A month later, when the grass was green and the flowers were blooming, the eggs began to hatch. The baby birds stuck their heads out from under their mother and demanded food.

The male owl worked harder than ever. He
flew about the tundra constantly, looking for
prey. This year there were more lemmings,
but there were also many more owlets to feed.

The female laid four eggs, and when they had all hatched she went hunting, too. Then the male owl was especially watchful. When he saw a jaeger near the nest, he dive-bombed it and chased it away. Once, when he saw a fox running in the direction of the nest, he flopped down on the ground nearby. He

dragged his wing, crying shrilly. He was pre-
tending that he had a broken wing. But the
fox wasn't fooled. He continued toward the
nest. Then the owl swooped down on the fox,
snapping at it with his beak. He stood on the
ground and glared and flapped his wings. The
fox turned and ran.

One by one, the little owlets grew strong and hopped out of the nest. Now they were harder to watch as they ran about the tundra and hid under the grass and low willows. But they all ran after the big owl when he flew down with food in his mouth. He tore the prey to pieces and gave some to each owlet. While they ate, he turned his head round and round, watching for enemies.

The days began to grow shorter again.
Darkness and cold were returning to the Arctic. The owl family moved south slowly. All
the owlets had learned to fly and to hunt. The
big white owl led his family toward the great
forests where he knew there would be food for
the winter. There the family separated. Each
owl found its own hunting ground. Some flew
farther south, looking for a better place to
hunt. But the big white owl stayed by himself
in the forest. He would not see his home again
till the sun returned, bringing spring to the
Arctic and another season of lemmings and
owlets to the tundra.

About the Author

ALICE L. HOPF is equally at home writing science fiction (under her maiden name, A. M. Lightner) and writing about nature. She is a member of the Lepidopterists Society, the New York Entomological Society, and the Audubon Society. She has written several other nature and animal books for Putnam's, among them *Biography of an American Reindeer, Biography of an Armadillo,* and *Biography of a Giraffe.*

About the Artist

FRAN STILES studied at Moore College of Art in Philadelphia and the Art Student's League in New York City. She has also been taught, she says, by the animals she has surrounded herself with and by those she has traveled to see. For a number of years she has worked as an illustrator for the American Museum of Natural History, where she studied wildlife under a grant from the New York State Council on the Arts. This is her first book for Putnam's.